ABOUT THE AUTHOR

Giovanni Esposito, better known as **SPOZ**, is a poet, writer, performer, musician and (mainly armchair) activist from Birmingham. He works a lot in schools as a poetry and 'slam poetry' workshop, and project, facilitator. He has written and produced plays and musicals for theatre and film and was Birmingham's Poet Laureate in 2006/7, which was nice. This is his second collection for a 15+ readership and has some older, previously unpublished work as well as lots of new stuff.

Also by SPOZ from VERVE Poetry Press - *Sometimes Angry,* 2019

Website: https://spoz.co/

To Charlotte...

Playful,
Poignant,
Pottymouth

Spoz

...enjoy!

VERVE
POETRY PRESS
BIRMINGHAM

PUBLISHED BY VERVE POETRY PRESS
https://vervepoetrypress.com
mail@vervepoetrypress.com

The right of Giovanni Esposito to be identified as author of this work has
been asserted in accordance with section 77 of the Copyright, Designs and
Patents Act 1988.

FIRST PUBLISHED MAY 2025

Printed and bound in the UK
by ImprintDigital, Exeter

ISBN: 978-1-913917-82-1

Cover illustration: Scott Tyrell

For Claudia, Francesca and Zack

CONTENTS

PLAYFUL

POIGNANT

POTTYMOUTH

Playful,
Poignant,
Pottymouth

Playful

Chris Packham's Really Ace

I really love that bloke to bits,
Midnight plays of punk rock hits,
Knows his finches from his tits,
Chris Packham's really ace.

He's our own English Naturalist,
His charm is quite hard to resist,
I might just have one off the wrist,
Chris Packham's really ace.

Keeps on fighting for the animals, all the plants and trees,
Trying to save the planet before it ends up on its knees,
He's a dedicated vegan so it's no to meat and cheese,
I bet his farts are fruity, so best crash out the Fabreeze!

Please, let's not be coarse, let's not be blunt,
But he won't like you if you hunt,
So stop it now you silly fools,
Chris Packham's really ace!

Chris Packham's really ace he is, Chris Packham's really ace,
He's an asset to the human race, Chris Packham's really ace!

He went to university,
Laughs in the face of adversity,
He loves bio diversity,
Chris Packham's really ace!

Don't harm a tree, a limb or leaf,
He might just give you loads of grief,
If you mess up a coral reef,
Chris Packham's really ace!

He gets up at the crack of dawn to sniff the morning dew,
He keeps us all so well informed with his nature driven crew,
Spring watch, Winter watch, Autumn, Summer too,
You can see him chuckle, talking tits both great and blue!

HS2 gets on his nerves,
There's no real purpose that it serves,
It's killing nature and reserves
Chris Packham's really ace!

Chris Packham's really ace he is, Chris Packham is the GOAT
He'll keep our earthly boat afloat, Chris Packham is the GOAT

He can't be beat, he can't be bought,
By the Countryside Alliance sort,
He'll sue their arses in a court,
Chris Packham's really ace!

Chris Packham's really ace he is, Chris Packham is the don
In the hit parade he's number one,
He'll cook your goose if you hurt a swan,
We'll bloody miss him when he's gone,
Chris Packham's really ace.

We're Birmingham … City

I've been a 'bluenose' since school (after a brief dalliance with Leeds United in the seventies, because they were winning lots). I was resident poet at Birmingham City FC for a few seasons in the noughties, which was great fun. Trying to sort that out again if I can. This poem appeared in one of the match day programs. We should have a resident poet at every football club … what d'yer reckon?

We're Birmingham …
Where neighbours help neighbours
Of different cultures and nations,
And with a little patience we begin to see
The beauty in our diversity.
And it comes as no surprise when you realise,
That our rich city is full of Mr. Blue Skies.
But we've got teeth …
You can see them when we grin,
We've got mats at our doors to welcome you in
To our neck of the woods …
Yeah … we've got rainbows in our neighbourhoods.

We're Birmingham …
Where sometimes, you've got to be a little bit naughty,
And UB40 give you food for thought,
About a fort built by Dunlop that lost its support
And remains in only name.
We've played the game, in fact, we've played a blinder,
And whenever we've felt peaky, we're here to remind you,
Write us off at your peril.
There's no bottom to our barrel so you can't scrape it,
We're the genuine article, 'cus Brum don't fake it.

We're Birmingham City …
Born of the Small Heath Alliance in 1875,
We began to thrive in the beautiful game

With a passion and drive and then a slight change of name ...
As bombs fell and hearts broke
And the streets filled with pain and pity,
We went from Small Heath ... to Birmingham ...
Then took the mantle of CITY!
Our second city pride that is second to none,
We dig in and battle and get the job done,
Legends have come and legends have gone,
But like that very long road ... we keep right on.

And when the opposition came and fancied their chances,
They came up against Latchfords, Gil Merrick and Francis,
They met their matches and to this day still do,
You may whine if you're claret but you sing if you're blue!
Our aim is true, like the right foot of Purse
Our memories tell stories like chapter and verse,
Packed Arsenal off in a Wembley hearse ...
We rode the blows ... left the gunners for dead,
With a gambol from Martins and Zigic's head,

So ... come Carrott, come Harewood, come bluenoses all,
Devotion's unleashed with the kick of a ball,
Let's nurture the seeds that our gaffer has sewed ...
And keep right on ... to the end of the road.

Limerick Verses Haiku
(A Poetic Match of the Day)

This was a five minute sketch I wrote and recorded for Radio Four's 'Ear Candy' programme back in 2004(ish), I think it was. I still have to apologise to Wales for the awful Welsh accent I put on during the recording. P.S. I just added a bit about VAR to bring it up to date a bit. It wasn't around back then!

Gary Baldy: sports' commentator
Ron De Valli: Welsh sports' commentator
Poet: the voice of the poet

Gary: Well, if you've just joined us, you have been missing one hell of a match. With a little under five minutes remaining on the clock, we have the score standing at Limerick 1, Haiku 1. It really has been end to end stuff hasn't it Ron?

Ron: Well yes Gary, it's been incredible hasn't it. We saw what the Japanese could do in the last world cup - and I tell you what, they've been showing us again today, with their traditional 5 – 7 – 5 formation, which, to be honest Gary, I never thought would be up to the task against the rhythmic, five line thrust of Limerick, but they've really given a good account of themselves here, today.

Gary: They certainly have Ron, but let's not count our chickens yet, because Limerick are breaking from midfield and it looks like they've got a man over...oh! Look at that!...

> Poet: An Aussie called Kylie Minogue,
> Was branded a bit of a rogue,
> At the drop of a hat,
> She would show you her bum,
> Though it got her a feature in 'Vogue'.

Gary: It's gone in...but, no, I don't think it's going to count, the linesman's waving his flag and there's going to be a VAR check too. I have to say Ron, I think I agree with them on this one.

Ron: Yes Gary, there was an infringement on the forth line. If we can have a quick look at that again...yes there it is. It should have gone...'at the drop of a hat, she would show you her...'

Gary: Yes Ron, a little blatant that one... and the ref's reaching for his pocket. Limerick have got their first yellow card of the game...well there are some tired legs out there.
Anyway ... the free kick's taken quickly by Haiku, can they come back with something special so late in the game? It's a lovely ball out to the left, he's round the defender – he shoots!...

> Poet: The fresh morning dew,
> Like pearls on a lush, green rug,
> Fade into nothing

Gary: Oh it's hit the post! It's come back out to Haiku for another shot at goal...

> Poet: The rainfall is warm
> Like an Indian summer
> but in Birmingham.

Gary: Oh, and that's easily gathered by the Limerick keeper. It bobbled a bit in front of Haiku there and he just couldn't get a good foot around it...and it's a good throw out to the right from the keeper, as Limerick begin to press forward again for what could be the last time in this match. They could have half a chance here...

> Poet: An astronaut en route to Venus
> Was blessed with a really large...

Gary: Oh, and Limerick nearly getting themselves into trouble there... and they've pulled it back to the half way line. It's the square ball to the left as Limerick throw everything forward here, they're leaving themselves open at the back – Haiku could catch them on the break if they're not careful. It's a firm, probing ball into the Haiku box. Limerick goes up...

> Poet: There was an old lady from Peckham,
> Who looked like Victoria Beckham,
> She wasn't that posh,
> 'Cause she had a moustache
> And if folks dared to point then she'd deck 'em!

Gary: Oh ! It's a terrific block from the keeper but Limerick are coming in for the rebound...

> Poet: There was an old grocer from Leek,
> Whose flatulent gases would reek,
> He cried 'Oh! My heart!'
> As he lit up a fart
> And blew himself into next week

Gary: It's there! Limerick have scored on the rebound in what must surely be the dying seconds of the game! Haiku are looking to the linesman for a flag ... but there isn't one. The VAR officials have had a look and have given the goal. And there's the final whistle, there isn't any time left to restart the game. Haiku can't believe it, the crowd can't believe and I must say Ron, I'm not sure if I believe it either.

Ron: Yes, Gary, It's pretty unbelievable...but as the Monkees once said 'I'm a believer' and I believe the score is Limerick 2, Haiku 1. Who'd have believed it.

Gary: Indeed Ron, couldn't have said it better myself. So there you have it, what can only be described as quite literally, 'the match of the day'. We leave it here in Madrid, at the 'Estadios de Palabras', Limerick 2, Haiku 1.

These Hills

I walk The Lickey Hills that straddle South Birmingham and North Worcestershire, quite often. I conducted a 'well being' project of walking and writing up there in 2024/25. This is something I wrote while the project participants were scribbling their poems and having their tea and biscuits.

These are the trees where real freedom lives,
Where nothing gives a fig about the mortgage or the bills,
Where the air fills lungs and lungs breathe it in,
Nature's free gym, where the woods begin.

These are the woods where sets and dens
Are hidden from the camera lens unless you really look.
Where a book will not tell you the full story
Of how this wood captured and caught me,
... how these hills enraptured and taught me,
Brought me a smile in spite of those who would taunt me.
Cleared the mind of thoughts that would haunt me.

These are the hills that get my heart pumping,
Beating and thumping like Animal drum fills,
No frills just feels, no infringement of copyright,
Feeling all the kills, like an encore on first night,
These are the hills where you see beyond eyesight.

We call you The Lickeys, though we're not sure why,
Your "Olde English" definition,
Seems to have passed a lot of us by,
But you can't deny you bear daily witness,
To a spring in the step and a load shedding sigh,
You were put here to enrich, to heal and to gratify.
You were here at my birth ...
... you'll be here when I die,
Because that's just the natural order of things,

When things are left to fly
With unclipped wings.

Friends When We Met

We were strangers when we met,
Though I'm sure I knew you ... I just didn't know it yet.
It doesn't make sense does it? Not many things did,
Situations were scary for this eighteen year old kid.
A friend of a friend made for a good excuse
To turn up where you might turn up too,
It's true ... yes, I know it sounds a little weird,
But I'd pluck up some courage ... and say "hello"...
Once the coast had cleared.

Were we strangers when we met?
Because we seemed to nest like Tetris blocks,
Seemed to be the long lost feet to our odd socks,
Meshing cogs in a gearbox of a well-oiled machine,
Seemed to feed our mental needs with a squirt of dopamine.
I was keen ... as a mustard cliché,
And even though my joints feel a little rusted these days,
I'll never forget the ribbons that we scissored at the start,
When you became the wizard
That gave this tin man a heart.

Goths in the Garden Centre

There were goths in the garden centre,
Were they looking for the blackest of roses?
They inhaled the fragrance of spring time blooms,
Through the piercings in their noses.

I'm not sure if they came here on purpose,
Or whether, in fact, they were lost,
Amidst the apple and cherry tree saplings,
And the 'three for two' bags of compost.

They were in their finest regalia,
Black skinny jeans and 'Nu Rocks'
They pondered over plants of red peppers,
That were priced at six pounds a box.

I wondered if they were part time vampires,
That drank the blood of their prey,
Or had they simply come for Begonias
That were on special offer that day.

Were they searching for white flowers of Hemlock?
Or the opium buds of the Poppy?
Or something to settle their tummies,
For when the cross channel crossing got choppy.

There was a beauty in their juxtaposed presence,
A joy in their pale, pallid hue,
They had a rainbow of flowers in their trolley,
Because graveyards need bedding plants too.

How Did You Get That Up There, Grandad?

To be read in a 'Pam Ayres' style voice (she too, is ace), except for the last line as Pam would never drop an 'F' bomb, would you Pam?

Senility may be creeping in,
Though you still have some wits about you...
And when you say that you had no assistance at all,
I have no reason to doubt you...

'Cause Grandma Joan has been dead a year now
And you have been living alone,
So how in God's name did you get that up there?
With no audible grumble or moan?

Your prize winning marrow has left you perturbed,
Your discomfort is hard to disguise,
'Cause an act such as that, for a man half your age,
Would have surely brought tears to one's eyes.

The size of the thing really beggars belief,
Just the thought makes me shudder and shriek,
If you'd tried to shove it up any higher, Grandad,
We'd be arranging your funeral next week!

I can smell just a hint of liniment...
Did you rub it well in just before
You attempted this act of sheer recklessness,
In the hope that you wouldn't be sore?

How did you get that up there, Grandad?
I hope that you don't tell the neighbours,
'Cause the word will get out and the press will come round,
To examine the fruits of your labours.

Grandad, you're all of a tremble,
Your kilter is on the decline,
Your complexion is pale, your fettle is frail,
I may have to call 999

To an old man in your fragile condition,
Such an act must have smarted and stung,
You're a testament to human persistence,
'Cause that's the best fucking picture you've hung.

The Night I Found Love on the Ladypool Road

As Birmingham's poet laureate, back in 2006/7, I was often asked to write and read at community events. I wrote this for an event at The Amanah Centre in Sparkhill, Birmingham which was attended by loads of people from the Muslim, Irish, Hindu and migrant communities. I remember the food was gorgeous and how similar our respective stories were. Lovely food, lovely people. I think they liked the poem too.

I was languishing in limbo, listless and limp,
With a ravenous rumble inside,
I was in need of sublime satisfaction,
My hunger was too hard to hide.

Like a wanderer from Wolverhampton,
Like a waif, a stray, an intruder ...
I was lost in the Balti Triangle,
About 3000 miles north/east of Bermuda.

I was drawn to a street where the lights were bright
And with a sense of purpose I strode,
Hoping tonight would be the night,
I'd find love on the Ladypool Road.

I was quickly seduced by your Punjab Paradise,
And pulled lovingly into your bosom,
By a man who spoke of your earthly delights
And an off license owned by his cousin.

I longed for the warm roundness of your vessel
And within minutes you were sprawled in front of me,
With your cascade of coriander, cardamom and cumin,
And more than just a cheeky squirt of ghee.

My senses were smitten, my craving aroused,
I was grateful that we were ... alone,
For I knew that your pieces of chicken,
Were exclusively ... off the bone.

So I dipped my naan ... and I dipped it again
And again and again and again ...
Onion or garlic, keema, peshwari,
Though tonight I had chosen one plain.

You made my trembling top lip moist,
My brow was furrowed and sweaty,
With my appetite sated, I grinned a broad grin,
Like the first time I saw Shilpa Shetty

My heart was lost, the deed had been done,
You had become another one of my vices,
I thanked God for Adil's and his Birmingham Balti,
With his secret blend of herbs and spices.

Science with Miss Davis

I wrote this for The Cheltenham Science Festival Poetry Slam back in 2008 (ish) and scraped through to the second round. I then went on to win it with "Love Letter to Jeremy Clarkson" in round two and "Dying for a Dump in the Car Back From Cheltenham" in the final. Who knew a science audience would have a thirst for such highbrow literature!

In seventy seven, science seemed tough,
Third year seniors and I'd had enough,
It was boring old stuff ... taught by gruff, Mr. Turner,
Who had the charm and the wit of an old Bunsen Burner.

His experiments with Nitrogen, well ... they just left me cold
And he smelt like a Petri dish covered with mould.
If B.O. was a show, he'd get the top billin'
And his lab coat arm pits encouraged growth of penicillin.

His tiresome tone was bad tempered yet tepid
And his blueprint for learning was less than intrepid.
My energy in science was lacking potential
And my growth of disinterest was near exponential.

I couldn't help messin' in my science lesson,
And the answers to questions? Well – I'd just be guessin'
Like those faltering flat lines on cardiograms,
I could feel ... myself failing ... my science ... exams _____ .

Then ... it happened ... at the start of the new term,
Mr. Turner was "terminated" like an H1N2 germ,
Like sperm lost en route in fallopian tubes,
Our new teacher started ... but this one had boobs.

Miss Davis ... oh ... Miss Davis,
I'm not really sure how to say ... this ...

But was there more than chemistry between me and you?
I know there was Physics and some Biology too...
Your theories on evolution were Darwin-esque
And your arse looked fantastic bent over the desk.

As we examined potassium and water effervescing,
My corrupted young mind did some mental undressing,
Your drip ... drip ...
Dropping of alkaline in acid,
Turned parts of my anatomy to the opposite of flaccid.

Do you remember that time you dissected a frog?
And the whole of the class ran to puke in the bog?
There was just you and I left alone in the lab,
You turned and said "Spoz, do you fancy a stab?"

My legs turned to jelly, I went all of a quiver,
How was I to know you meant the dissected frog's liver?
I lunged forward on the error of judgement I'd made,
And impaled myself on your sharp scalpel blade.

I still bear the scars, though Miss Davis, it's true,
My scraping a "C" was all down to you.

The Rotunda Quatrains

I wrote this in response to a prompt from Julie Boden (RIP bab x) back in 2005, who said "Write something about Brum in quatrains, with the first three lines rhyming and the fourth being a repeating refrain of eleven syllables". I do like a tight form. This poem helped me get the Brum Poet Laureate gig the following year.

Rotunda – carbuncle or architectural icon?
Is it like a bike rack without a single bike on?
A platter of oysters? Though you can't say you'd like one.
Blunder? Eighth wonder? The Brummie Rotunda

Like a gigantic 'Smartie' tube stuck on it's end,
This robust Rotunda will drive you round the bend,
Oblivious to bombs the IRA used to send,
Blunder? Eighth wonder? The Brummie Rotunda

Profound or profane this cylindrical frame?
A product of genius from a brilliant young brain?
Or is it the drug engulfed sixties that are really to blame?
Blunder? Eighth wonder? The Brummie Rotunda

Derided at first, now a place in our hearts,
The point at which Birmingham both ends and starts
A defiant two fingers to the old arty farts
Blunder? Eighth wonder? The Brummie Rotunda

From bottom to top, every inch is a gem
Our own Eiffel Tower, it's our crème de la crème,
I bet every Londoner says, "Wish we 'ad one of them!"
Blunder? Eighth wonder? The Brummie Rotunda

Lockdown Valentine's Day

I'll try to be your flint, if you think you need a spark,
I'll even try to be your 'two by two' as we're boarding Noah's Ark,
If you have a castle in the air, then I'll try to help you see it,
But with the kind of year that we've been having ...
I'm afraid I just can't guarantee it.

Because, this is not just any old Valentine's Day,
And this is most definitely not a Mark's and Spencer Valentine's Day,
(Other posh food retail outlets are available),
No ... this is, hopefully, a once in a lifetime Valentine's Day,
Never to be repeated,
So if you're feeling a bit deflated and defeated,
I'll try to be your "pick me up" ... your Tiramisu,
Your ... "Not that great, but making do",
Your ... "I don't think it's Covid, it's more like the flu,
But let's hug anyway, because, wild thing ... I think I love you"

It's true.

I may not be your first choice at the front of the queue,
Though, like an intrepid Brummie once said ... "I'll give it a goo".

Last year was a tragic and worrying one for many a folk,
It seemed like our collective futures were going up in smoke.
But our hopes and dreams are still in range,
We could do with a few ch ... ch ... ch ... changes
As we turn and face the strange.
Everything will be hunky dory once again,
Well ... as hunky dory as it was before-y,
Never leave health issues in the hands of a Tory,
And let's hope it doesn't drag on like

some

kind

                           of

                                shaggy

                                     dog

                                          story.

Anyway ... back to this lockdown Valentine's Day.
Celebrate it, if you wish, in any and every way you may,
Have a take away or cook, have a 'play' or read a book
And be sure you're more than ready before you ask,
Because if you're going to lean in for a Valentine's kiss ...
You'll need to remove your mask.

I Wanna Be Jaws

*So ... yeah ... you'll spot the form (and title) similarities
to a John Cooper Clarke poem here. Well ... he's bleedin'
ace isn't he? One of the many reasons why I got into
poetry, so why not?*

I wanna be your big Bond villain,
With massive shiny teeth,
I will bite your cable car cable in half,
Because my gob's beyond belief.
If you like scaring kids a lot,
Let my knashers hit the spot,
They never rot,
I wanna be Jaws.

I wanna start off as a bad guy,
Then turn good when I fall in love,
I want to be your iron fist,
Wrapped up in a velvet glove.
I would go to any length,
With my super human strength,
I'm your better tenth,
I wanna be Jaws.

I wanna be a fishy predator,
That you'll need a bigger boat for,
I want to be your yellow barrel,
So you and I can float more,
You'll be safe upon my ship,
I'll never take your leg off at the hip,
Just get a grip,
I wanna be Jaws.

I wanna be your latex great white shark,
I'll take all the harpoons,
I'll sing you "Show Me the Way to Go Home"
And a hundred other sea themed tunes,
I'll be the drama and commotion,
Around Amity and the Atlantic Ocean,
You won't need no sun tan lotion,
I'll move with a slightly unnatural motion,
I wanna be Jaws.

Poignant

Got Any Change?

Blanked ... like the elephant in the gloom, or in the park,
Or in the doorway that's invisible to all but a handful.
You carry your mantle handed down by hearts of stone,
Who cast off your skin and bone,
Like a careless absent parent's responsibility.

A society built on the backs of fragility,
And when our leaders lack the ability to care and take action,
We will see that homeless fraction turn into double figures.
We will hear the taunts and sniggers of
"Druggie" and "Get a job",
We will feel the frost bitten boot at kicking out time,
As drunken wife beaters stumble to their humble abodes.
We will smell the trickle down economy,
Like the empty bladders of hedge fund managers.
We will taste the bitterness of frustration,
As another day drags...
Gasping for fags...
Twenty four hour beds of sleeping bags.

Gemma faces her daily dilemma.
Does she run the gauntlet of her mom's abuse and dirty looks,
Or take her overnight chances under the canopy of Starbucks?
(Other tax dodging canopies are available).
Does Tom head back to watch his mom
Take another smack on the chin,
Before his well hammered dad turns on him?
Or take the grim, yet relative safety of the derelict shack
Round the back of the garages?

And while the government tells us of a winning plan,
The uncomfortable truth will flush the spin down the pan.
How can we watch so many ships crash against rocks,

Before they're moored in the safety of their harbours and docks?
Strung up in stocks because you placed an "X"
In the wrong box ... the box of 'us' neglecting 'them',
That will condemn young souls to be tossed aside,
Like spare change or a bad penny,
Knowing full well, that one homeless life,
Is one forgotten life too many.

Flagpoles in the Garden
(Nothing in the Fridge)

They feed their kids on bigotry burgers,
They magiced out of thick air.
Someone told them it was patriotic
To jeer at people from "over there",
To feel anger and rage at their despair,
To sneer at those who appear to care.

There's only so much hate you can consume
Before it becomes all consuming,
"Hand me down" grooming
Of kids who are kids of the kids
Of when babies were booming.

And when there's an election looming,
The menu will serve cold, tasteless dishes ...
Division instead of unity,
Poison speech, labelled as "free",
Fear mongers for fish and entitled impunity.

Their forefather's follies were rewarded as cannon fodder,
Cap doffed for a flag, and any political slag,
That wrapped themselves in it,
As armour against criticism of corruption.
Another line of production and industrial wheels
Making gullible fools and imbeciles,
Striking deals with a lobby that profits from pain,
Placing Johnny Foreigner in the line of fire again.

And it's always been like this.

The bread lines are turned into battle grounds,
Where punching down is just another warm pint
In the Hare and Hounds.
Pockets of pennies that used to be pounds.
Then a stagger through the subway,
And a totter over the bridge,
And home to flagpoles in the garden
And nothing in the fridge.

Duvet Day

All I did today was get out of bed ... for a bit.
I felt like shit and then felt like cack,
So after a coffee ... I went straight back.
The devious draw of the duvet can be hard to resist,
Warm and intoxicating, if you get my gist?
A shelter in the murky mist,
A must for Mondays or times like this,
A bliss to bless when your head's bereft.

You're my fifteen tog jacket that's not as straight
As the one I think might fit me best.
Did I need the extra rest?

Nah.

But you know what? Fuck it.
While I detest the distress caused by this uninvited guest,
I will languish in the knowledge
That I will be fine if I remain undressed.
I will be fine if I'm a little bit smelly,
I will be fine if all I watch is shit daytime telly,
I will be fine if all I eat is ice cream and...

... more ice cream.

I will lie there in my downy downess and daydream,
I will scroll through feel good meme after feel good meme,
I will let out a scream as I wish I could punch
The person who posted "Happiness is a journey, not a destination"...

Thank you Dalai fucking Lama.
I will feel better, I will feel calmer,
So cancel the undertaker and the embalmer,

The drama will end and I will feel okay,
But for now...

Let's file today...

Under C.B.A.

Dying For a Day in November

And in the laying down of their lives, lay hope ... or so they
were told.
The hopes of nations and future generations.
Generations who may tip their hats and doff their caps,
Though will ultimately fail to grasp,
Or abhor the horror of war.

War, in all its false glory.
For as the berets are tossed skyward,
The tears will tell a different story,
Of forefathers who have gone before me.
Gone to the volley of a rifle salute,
The very rifles that shoot for a new dawn,
Though turn to folly as new governments are born
Out of indifference to our differences,
Build walls with barbed wire fences
And terrorise their people by pumping the fear in,
Like a runaway truck without any steering.

So how many more flags will we drape over coffins or burn in
the streets?
How many more sobs and bleeding hearts,
Before someone starts to abstain from brandishing words of
such weight
That are tossed so lightly?
And consider a world that could be – just might be?
Free from all fighting? Hmm ... not bloody likely...
As long as the silent majority
Keep going 'over the top' into the 'no man's land' of insanity,
Will humanity fail to feel the warm duvet of peace,
Like a quilted fleece on a November morning ...
Warming ... from the outside, in.
It's a sin to suppose that war's the solution

To evolution at different paces,
To different skin on different faces,
To different Gods in high places -
Let's pack our cases ... and move to another planet,
Conflict is a fire and there's always money to fan it
With narrow-mindedness and intolerance, from all sides.
Bridge those divides - we should strive to endeavour
That the backwardness of war's raw edge ... is sheathed
... forever.

Pigs in Banquets

This is written as a song and if you scan the QR Code at the end, it will take you to a YouTube video where I do the singy chorus parts (multi tracked harmonies and stuff) and my great friend and mentor, Dreadlockalien, is toasting the verses. If the QR Code doesn't work, just look for "Pigs in Banquets with Spoz and Dreadlockalien", in YouTube, should do the trick. I hope I got the patois right (ish).

Chorus :
See them pigs ... pigs in banquets,
See them pigs ... pigs in banquets,
Dem be spitting 'pon de working man,
While him robbing all de coin he can,
See those pigs ... pigs in banquets.

Pigs in banquets ... dem got dem snout in da trough,
Corruption and lies, yeah dey just brush it off,
Dem laugh and dem scoff, doff dem cap and dem cough,
Tek scraps from de table of de Czar Romanov

Pigs in banquets ... you keep voting dem in,
Me laugh at democracy, me laugh at de spin,
Dividing our kin so de pigs always win (remember),
You are ma sista, you are ma bredrin.

Pigs in banquets ... too much blood dat dey spill,
Rejoice in de selling of de weapons dat kill,
Dem thrill at da million, dem can't get dem fill,
Truth and justice is their bitterest pill

Pigs in banquets ... what make dem tick?
Dey hide behind deception and da bad politricks,
Dem slick in their clique, we need to mash it up quick,
Line dem all up and give 'em nuff licks!

Pigs in banquets ... compassion is gone,
Dem fill your heart with dread lookin' after number one,
Dem turning Zion to de evil Babylon,
Dem like a bruk record, dem go on and on

Pigs in banquets ... dem mekin' me sigh,
Dem tell me 'All Lives Matter' but won't look me in de eye,
Always asking 'why?' when we mek de hue and cry,
With dem knee pon my neck, till the I and I die.

Scan to view video on YouTube

See What You Want to See

Is that what you think it is?
Is that someone waving or drowning?
Are you thinking really hard or simply frowning?
Scowling at the thought of an island's overcrowding?
Or figuring out how you can help,
Before someone throws the towel in?

Are you looking at a nightmare or a vision?
Getting a reasoned result after your own inquisition?
Or following somebody else's twisted mission,
That makes you gag on an 'oven ready' decision?
Saving lives ... or another dangerous imposition?

Which is it?

Are you witnessing an invasion?
Or does their different colour and cultural persuasion
Provide the wrong answer to a simple equation?
Two plus two does not equal five,
However hard you may contrive to make it so.
Yet you always try to fake it though.
But every formula or statistic you attempt to apply
Will always make it a lie, so why try?
Why try to deceive, unless it's you who's on the make?
Why try to divide, just to snatch a fatter slice of the cake?

You see? That's the thing with opinions,
They're a distorted reality of our mental ability,
That's laced with our own strengths and fragility...
You see what you want to see.
Perhaps they're a measure of our own standards?
Do we play it safe or are we chancers?
Do we move to the tune of aspiring puppet masters?

Are we human or are we dancers?
And do opinions provide more questions than answers?

The Times They Are a Changed

Have you been furloughed or just laid off?
Caught a bit of Covid or just have a nasty cough?
Are you Emo or Goth?
Are you even surprised?
Or has your outlook been sanitised
By another prospect of shielding and self isolation?
Are you following the science or an alternative education?
Can you see the rays of sunshine
Through the darkness and gloom?
Will your next poetry gig be 'in the flesh' or over 'Zoom'?

Have you heard of herd immunity?
Are these unprecedented times an opportunity
For some real care in our community?
As our leaders act with apparent impunity?
So much stuff that's new to me, but is it new to you?
Will our kids know shit loads more than we will ever do?

Do you see what you want to see?
Are you anti vax because you prefer a Henry?
(other vacuum cleaners are available)
Are your deals 'oven ready' or just more fake news?
Do you stay to watch the firework display,
Or simply light the fuse?
Are you a sheep, a snowflake, gammon or woke?
Do you always miss the joke through the smoke of deceit?
Are you broke, like a record
Stuck on repeat?

Do you scream about rights to opinions
As long as they agree with yours?
Are you one of those 'freedom of speech' bores
With 'Chinese Whispers' as your evidence and proof?

Is yours the only truth?
And will you speak it to power?
Or will you hold the tap open for this corrupt shitshower?

The Aubergine Uber Gene

In times of austerity, poverty and hunger,
When the mackerel's full of mercury, down at the fishmonger,
And the ooze in the rivers might get you shouting "Cowabunga!"
Don't linger no longer and don't vent your spleen,
The future is here,
The answer is clear,
It's time for the aubergine uber gene.

Imagine an eggplant the size of a bus,
Imagine the ruckus, kerfuffle and fuss,
A moussaka so big it could feed all of us,
An abundance that's lean, mean and green,
Share the love, fruit and fibre,
Become a subscriber,
To this new cyber source of protein.

The aubergine uber gene, like a song from Encanto,
Like Matilda, the musical, like a Christmas time panto,
What a wonderful gift from our friends at Monsanto,
'Cause you know that their chemistry's clean,
You won't have to worry,
If there's a glow in your curry,
It's just the effects of the aubergine uber gene.

It beats a space hopper sized Brussel sprout
And a penis shaped parsnip, what's that all about?
Goodbye constipation and a farewell to gout,
You'll change your mind if you think mustard's keen,
It can't be decried,
Gene's been modified,
The GM aubergine uber gene.

We won't need Live Aid to feed the world,
So put up the bunting, get the flags unfurled,
Last time Bob Geldof sang, my fucking hair curled!
It's on the menu of every café and canteen.
If there's fire in your asses,
Due to noxious food gases,
It's the mutant cuisine,
Of the post Brexit dream,
Just like Soylent Green,
We can fuck food hygiene,
The obscene aubergine uber gene.

Seeing Through Gary

Gary was proper wankered before he got twatted,
And a friendly passer-by, put him in the recovery position.
But he would never, fully, recover.
Nor did he want to, by his own admission,
Because he needed something to hate,
It made him feel better, made him feel great,
Made it easier to relate to his "working class struggle",
Where he was the "pure blood" and they were the "muggle".

And the night had started off so well ...
Finding heaven in hell and a heap of trouble.
He was shot to pieces by the bottom of a dozen shot glasses,
And like witches at black masses, he got carried away ... again.
Convinced the sword was mightier than the pen,
Swinging at men who could see his mask falling
From a face that a mother had loved ...
That a father had never, truly, embraced
That an unconditional loyalty had misplaced,
That free speech had defaced ... what a waste.

And he was ... wasted.

His tongue that was tied, was casually unknotted,
Besotted with forty five percent proof,
A loud mouth spewing his perverted truth
To a colourful youth who had heard it all before ...
He knew the score and had tasted the bile,
Yet had kept a calm head when the air had turned hostile.

Until tonight.
He climbed down off the fence,
Rewarding "free speech" with something called "consequence"
Something Gary had avoided in his little clique,
With their numbers to hide in, for the ignorantly weak.

Seconds after the blow had kissed his cheek,
His head kissed the slabs,
The spilt guts of kebabs decorated the pavement
Like a slaughter house floor.
Kissed teeth turned a walked away,
And whilst Gary's head would hurt from this foul, justified display,
He would get to spout his free speech shite,
Another day.

Sum of a Preacher Man

In 2022, Birmingham hosted the Commonwealth Games. I was picked as one of six "Bards of Brum" for the opening ceremony. This was the poem that got me the gig by responding to a couple of George Dawson quotes:

"The time has come to give everything to everyone"
"The time of private ownership has, I hope, nearly come to an end"

You should google him, he was pretty decent for his time.

In a time when socialism was being a radical liberal,
A preacher man's tongue could be measured ... yet visceral,
Every single syllable was revolutionarily biblical,
"The time has come to give everything to everybody" ...
Yeah ... I'm still a little cynical.

Birmingham would have been up the creek without Dawson,
He was awesome ...
And if the fairest of hands weren't being dealt for the workers,
Then he'd force 'em,
Well ... not force exactly ... more like cajoling,
A bit like Moeen Ali and his right arm off-spin bowling,
Loosening the grip of the controllers' controlling,
Shakespeare for the masses?
Our George got the ball rolling.

He got the big doors open and they're still open now,
Though we've watched the beaten brow of the small ones close
And who knows? If George was around today ...
He'd be rallying the righteous down at Smallbrook Queensway,
He'd be celebrating rainbows with the great and the good,
He'd be partying hard in our beautiful 'gaybourhood'.
He'd have the student fees on their knees,
In every West Midland university,
He'd be cheering on the three degrees

And our cultural diversity.
He'd be a thorn in the side of those calling him a menace,
He'd be telling the world ... we've got more canals than Venice!

So raise a glass or doff your cap to Brum Town's unsung friend,
"The time of private ownership has, I hope, nearly come to an end"
And with that tragic irony ...
He gave us books and dreams to get lost in,
For the many ... not the few ...
George Dawson ... you were bostin.

There Always Seems To Be Room For Dessert

They whinge and whine and moan
About the tax they're asked to pay,
While waiting times at A&E have gone up to a day,
"5% for JSA?
There really is no fucking way!"
Their future floats on your decay,
So keep your aspirations in the dirt,
Are you listening to what I'm saying?
There's no way that they'll be paying,
And there always seems to be room for dessert.

The down at heel sink further down,
That's the way the system's made,
A lobby's crafty bung is how the filthy scum get paid,
Another procedure been delayed,
'Cause government failed to make the grade,
But attention is so easy to divert,
Just point at immigrants on them boats,
That'll get you loads of votes,
And there always seems to be room for dessert.

I wonder when humanity became a political pawn?
I wonder when compassion became a word to scorn?
Children die, mothers mourn,
It's been like this since they were born,
You're doomed today and here comes the dawn,
So smile amidst the suffering and hurt,
It's not genocide, it's slaughter,
As they stop your food and water,
And there always seems to be room for dessert.

Peace, love and understanding's
Been switched for bitterness and rot,
Why are we not nurturing the beauty that we've got?
Have our leaders lost the plot,
Aboard their million dollar yacht?
The truth ain't hard to see if you're alert,
A handful stay delighted,
When us plebs are not invited,
And there always seems to be room for dessert.

Another Letter to Birmingham

Dear Birmingham,

What the fuck have you been playing at?
What the fuck has gotten into your head?
You've always been a little bit shit, but now you've gone and shit the bed ...
Upped sticks and fled,
Leaving the ragged trousered to lie in the shit instead.

You've been taken for a fool by shit men on a manky mission,
And by your own volition, you've let it happen,
Kept kicking the can down the streets ...
The very streets that are filled with neglected apparitions
And empty acts of contrition that are just that ... acts,
While the easy streets of a prosperous postcode
Provides proportionately less to shoulder the load.

We've been keeping right on to the end of the road,
But fucking hell it's a long one,
And when it feels like all hope is gone,
Bitter eyes turn right and believe the shite from a grifter's mouth,
Quenching thirsts in the dearth and drought,
Promises of with, to those without.

And they fall for it ... every time.

Blinkered by boats they cry, "Who needs a library anyway!?"
You may as well burn the books that you snatch from the hands
Of the folk on the beeches of Frankley.
The narrative's rank and their reasoning's wanky,
Pass me a hanky as I weep for the kids and teens
Of a library closure in Bartley Green,
Boldmere, Sutton Coldfield, Glebe Farm and Walmley,

And the irony isn't lost on me,
As the penny wise, pound foolish,
Home in on Bloomsbury.

I watch white elephants grow on your landscape,
As you pathetically ape cities you're not even coming second to.
So many downtrodden keep on looking up to you,
Waiting for your neo liberal economy to trickle down.
But it's like Thatcher's tears ... they only trickle down for herself,
So you'll keep on squandering rather than sharing the wealth.

And there really is a lot of it about ... wealth, that is.

Just check out the prices on Ozzy's final huzzah!
Villa Park mayhem with Tony's riffing, Brum built guitar.
They're charitable geezers though, and Bill's back, like their beginnings,
"Paranoid" played on an SG by John Diggins.

Birmingham ... I've seen you do it a thousand times.
Patching up unmitigated disasters,
With a damp paper towel and sticking plasters.
Kick out those bastards and kick out the jams,
We're sick of the scams that our strugglers have to subsidise
And it's no surprise when we see
The right wings of vultures unfurl before our eyes,
What did you expect?
Your hooded knight is branding you "serf",
And denying us seeds for our fertile earth,
Ignoring our worth, when his breed needs to be mounting their steeds
And slaying those dragons of division and greed,
Instead of giving them a leg up.

I love you Brum ... you know I do,
And if I sound pissed off, it's 'cause I am,
I'm angry at what you've let yourself become,
Gruel for too many ... fresh Lobster for some.

You gave me a voice and you make dreams achievable,
With our drawn out vowel sounds and extra syllables,
You're real and believable, but it really grates,
When you trade your greatness for mediocrity,
Let's have a change of philosophy,
Not every world beating team has to be led by Socrates ...
Let them all scoff ... we could have Dino Zoff.

And when we win the UK's worst accent award
For the umpteenth consecutive year,
I'll be sure to shout it loud and clear,
For those at the back ...
And for those down here ...
Do better Birmingham,
I *know* ... you can do better.

Pottymouth

Love Letter to Jeremy Clarkson
(It's Okay, I'm Only Joking)

Dear Scummy Jeremy, son of Clark,

Do you get dressed in the dark?
If you were on my ship, I'd have to disembark,
Petrol in your veins? Here ... let me inject a spark.

Clarkson, you embody everything that's crap with humanity,
When I think of you, my speech turns to
Extreme, obscene profanity ...
You fucking twat ... you see?
It happens quite a lot,
When your parents had you, they should have had you ... shot,
Was it them who taught you,
That obnoxiousness was best?
Clarkson you're a piece of shit ... I'm glad I got that off my chest!
You impose your piss-poor opinions,
With your laddish, bully boy tactics,
Be friends with you? I'd rather chew
Some second hand prophylactics.

You're a blatant fucking misogynist ... it's an infuriating trait,
I bet you think of big fast cars when you masturbate.
You spout your bile and toxic shite then say ... "But I was only joking!"
I'm sure there's no sound that's quite as sweet,
As you and Piers Morgan choking.
You've become a spokesman for farmers
From Penzance to Shetland to Dover,
Which is ironic when one realises it's twats
Like you who've been fucking them over!
You're nothing but a fossil, like the fuel you like to burn,
Take this Skoda for a spin and please do not return.
I know you don't like Birmingham,

Well frankly I don't care,
It's not a patch on your Oxfordshire home,
So stay the fuck down there.
Your tiresome schoolboy racial slurs and your right wing rhetoric,
Makes me want to beat you with a great big fuckin' stick!
You're arrogant, you're bigoted, you're self absorbed and blunt
You chauvinist,
You anus,
You total nob,
You cunt.

Assisted Dying for the Terminally Shite

For every stupid adult who calls their sleeping wear "jimjams"
For every bore who prefers Mariah Carey's Christmas song to Wham's,
For every so called grown up who calls their holiday "holibobs",
For every dopey rioter attacking Greggs with angry mobs,
For every person squeezing from the middle of toothpaste tubes,
For every uninvited groper of arses, dicks and boobs,
For every selfish person who sets off fireworks well after midnight,
Bring on assisted dying for the terminally shite.

For every dirty bastard who pisses in the sink,
For every fucking wanker who spikes a person's drink,
For every serial killer with corpses in their garage,
For every Tommy Ten Names, Enoch Powell and fucking Farridge,
For every Clarkson devotee who says "He tells it how it is"
For every scummy dealer selling children Es and Whizz,
For every far right fucking twat who says "Not far right ... just right",
Bring on assisted dying for the terminally shite.

For every gobby "Karen" who should keep their cakeholes shut,
For every fucking racist who says "I'm not racist, but ..."
For every tax dodging millionaire, who believes they are exempt,
For every twat who uses "woke" as an expression of contempt,
For every git on horseback taking packs of dogs to hunt,
For every naive bellend supporting Donald Trump, the cunt,
For every health care CEO delaying treatment day and night,
Bring on assisted dying for the terminally shite.

For every neoliberal, who has no morals, plainly,
For every nasty human who treats animals inhumanely,
For every hasbara troll, justifying slaughter in Palestine,
For every fucking bastard sending children down a mine,
For every politician who fiddles their expenses,
For every "free speech" advocate, who refutes the consequences,

When a sunken refugee dinghy is met with cheers and delight,
It's time for assisted dying for the terminally shite.

Bad Diet

I've got rubble in my tradesman's entrance,
I've been treating it just like a fool,
I've been getting a lot of discomfort,
When I've dropped the kids off at the pool.
My diet's been all out of balance,
I've been skipping on my fruit and veg,
Like a poorly trained furniture maker,
My stools have been rough round the edge.

That vindaloo I ate the other night,
Washed down with five or six "Carlings",
Came flying out the very next day,
Like a flock of fucking starlings.
Treat your anus with respect
And you know it'll respect you back,
Treat it like a shit hole
And it'll make you feel like cack.

Exercise some self restraint,
It's a very simple thing,
Or your arse will look like a beaten up boxer...
... Bloody around the ring.
So say "No!" to that quarter pound burger,
Throw that kebab out with the litter,
'Cause at the end of the day, a bad diet doesn't pay...
But it pays to be good to your shitter.

Morrison's Have Run Out of Lettuce

Morrison's have run out of lettuce!
Oh what the fucking hell!?
Morrison's have run out of lettuce!
It looks like Brexit's going well.

Morrison's have run out of lettuce,
So have Sainsbury's and Tesco's too,
I wanted a bit on my sandwich,
Now what the fuck am I supposed to do?

I'd have loved a bit of chopped up Iceberg,
Some Little Gem or some Cos,
I would have laid them, undressed, upon my bread,
Preceded by a satisfying toss.

I'm sorry if you think I'm being overly dramatic,
In the writing of this angry ballad,
But when you're missing leaves of Lollo Rosso,
How the fuck do you make a continental salad?

"Grow your own", I hear you say,
With your sanctimoniously brilliant green fingers,
Well, I can't tell the difference between
Cress and fucking stingers!

Oh! What I'd give to get my hands on a bit,
But I don't think that I can,
Though Elton John is doing fine,
'Cause he's a Rocket man.

Nasty Letter To … (Insert Name Here)

I get upset when I think of you,
Your name alone can spoil my day,
I'd like to give you a one way ticket to the moon,
But it just isn't far enough away.

You're as sought after as thrush…you're as pleasant as scabies,
I'd like to lock you in a room with a dog that's got rabies,
They should have cut your cock and bollocks off, to stop you making
babies,
I've never seen a queer wasp, but I've seen a lot of gay bees.

You see! You make me think irrational thoughts; you really do my
head in,
You're like a big turd in the swimming pool or a spurned 'ex' at a
wedding.
You're a law unto yourself; I wish you'd terminate your health,
Why don't you stand beneath that anvil perched, precariously, on that
shelf?

There's nothing that can compensate for everything you lack,
If you only cost a penny then I'd want my money back.
Do you know you've traumatised thousands of happy and fulfilled lives?
Just do us all a favour mate and juggle these 'Stanley' knives.

I'd like to hug you like a bear would – give you a big 'Glaswegian kiss',
But you're like a swollen prostate - two drops short of a piss.
I'd like to help you build a patio and bury you under the slabs,
You have the charm and wit and elegance of a nasty dose of crabs.

You're a 'Prince Albert' gone septic – the strobe when I'm epileptic,
At the infant school nativity play, you're the overly vocal sceptic.

You're as welcome as Jimmy Saville at a mother and toddler group,
You take Shiatsus with the shits for walks and forget the pooper scoop.

If your temperament were a vegetable,
Then you'd border on a 'cauli',
You're like a fumbled piece of shopping...completely off your trolley.
You're a glass and a half of monkey spunk,
In a bowl of Angel Delight,
If only your dad had had a wank instead,
Then I wouldn't have had to write this shite.

Swearing

Swearing isn't big, swearing isn't clever,
Swearing can be a consequence of one's fruitless endeavour,
But when you're born in Birmingham,
Which can sometimes be quite scary,
Then swearing forms a great big part
Of one's vo – cab – u – lary.

Now, swearing can be colourful,
Or even poetic, if it's mastered,
'Cause there's something deep and meaningful
In 'piss', 'fuck', 'shit', 'wank', 'bastard'.
Swearing's sometimes unavoidable,
Especially in DIY,
Like when you're trying to assemble those flat packed shelves,
From IKEA or MFI.
There're missing screws and bits don't fit,
Or some other warehouse blunder,
And the instructions look like they've been drawn
By Stevie fuckin' Wonder.

Swearing's often frowned upon and "politically incorrect",
But I was born in Birmingham, so what the fuck do you expect?
"Crikey! Oh bother! Fiddlesticks!" you say?
Is your temper tempered with that?
Get the anger out of your system,
With a "FUCKING BOLLOCKS" you twat!

Sometimes other words just won't do
To convey emotion or mood,
A considered and well placed "C" bomb,
Will give the impact to which you allude.

So...remember that swearing can cut you,
Like a razor that's sharpened to shave on,
But it's ever so hard, to talk like the bard,
When you're from Brum and not Stratford on Avon.

The Day I Caught my Foreskin in my Flies

T'was a morning much like any other,
As I began to sense my erection,
It must have been the new Kay's catalogue,
Well, specifically...the lingerie section.

I sped off to the gents at a purposeful pace,
With my trusty new Kay's catalogue,
Then in cubicle five, I did the 'hand jive'
And started cranking one off in the bog.

No sooner had I got out my member,
I felt my cubicle door take a push,
So I coughed and I fumbled and leant back on the door
And then yanked up my zip in a rush.

'Pain' was such an inadequate word,
To express the distress that I felt,
As I let out a scream that only dogs could hear
And could make the North Pole fucking melt.

I looked down at my tattered and torn chunk of flesh,
It was throbbing all pink, red and blue,
I wept like only a grown man could weep
And wished that I'd been born a Jew.

My foreskin was caught, my senses were fraught,
It looked like a mangled old kipper,
There was nothing else for it, so before anyone saw it,
I yanked down that nasty old zipper.

I winced and then blarted, I shat and then farted,
I wailed and I swore and I cursed,
My uncle John Thomas was battered and bruised
And my bollocks were near fit to burst.

I staggered on out of the cubicle,
With my foreskin and nob weeping puss,
I headed on down to the high street,
Where I jumped on the first fucking bus.

As I burst through the doors of casualty,
My predicament just got a lot worse,
'Cause as I stood at reception to book myself in,
I thought 'How the fuck do I explain *that* to the nurse'.

The Turd That Wouldn't Flush

This is based on a true story. Not mine, I hasten to add.

Our glances met across the room
My heart – it skipped a beat
She was all that I'd dreamt a woman could be
From her head right down to her feet

I licked my finger – and wiped my brow
She giggled and started to blush
If only I'd known that she'd be the owner
Of the turd that wouldn't flush

We went back to her place and with a smile upon her face
She said 'Do you fancy a coffee?'
I said 'I'd rather sample your muffin, my dear'
She said 'Cherry, Choc-Chip or Banoffee?'

Her teasing hands wandered, her pleasing lips kissed
The blood raced to my nob with a "whoosh"
Though later, it would drain like a water filled sink
When I found the turd that wouldn't flush

We fumbled with buttons and straps on the floor
I knew we'd be at it real soon
Though my bladder was aching and near fit to burst
So I asked 'Where's the little boys' room?'

'First on the left' she said, teasing me further
'I'll be waiting right here, don't be long'
As she puckered her lips and undid some more zips
And longingly whipped off her thong

So I raced down the hall and took the first left
I burst through the door with a push
I whipped out my 'old man' and stared down at the pan
And found the turd that wouldn't flush

As I pissed on the log, I started to grin
Forming pictures of her as she shat
I finished my piss and went back in the room
And then opened my gob like a twat

'We've captured a passionate moment' I said
'And I honestly don't want to spoil it,
But since you live alone, I just wanted to know
Is that your massive shit down the toilet?'

Her face glowed bright red, her embarrassment grew
I felt like a sorry old whimp
She started to sob and that's when my nob
Went all wobbly and flaccid and limp

The moment was lost by my foolish jape
She put on her clothes in a rush
She flung *mine* in my face then flung *me* out the door
All because of the turd that wouldn't flush.

Rubery Tuesday

Just in case you don't know, Rubery is a village that crosses the South Birmingham / Worcestershire border, on the A38, close to Junction 4 of the M5. It also happens to be where I was born and where I grew up. Big up the B45 massive!

Hello ... good evening ... ociffer,
I hope my drunken breath is not too sinful,
But I can assure you of my testimony,
Even though I've had a skinful.
A brimfull ... just a thimble or more or less,
I wasn't keeping score after an hour or so,
I'm sorry ... I digress.

I saw it all as clear as night, with my intoxicated vision,
But you can count upon my account,
Like any trusted politician ... ha! Of course I jest!
I'll nail a few brass tac facts
Then, sort of, fill in all the rest.

So ... yeah ... yer see cuntstubble,
I was in The Neighbourhood,
My kind of hostelry ... an ambience of sandalwood,
Makes you feel good as you sip
And lick the rum from off your lip.
Let me skip to the point ...
Someone must've been toking on a joint,
'Cause there was a whiff of weed,
Now I know the conspiracy theorist on the corner
Grows the stuff from seed ... you seen his attic?
His behaviour's quite erratic ... can be dramatic,
Robustly emphatic with his opinions expressed as facts ...
And he loves the smell of Chemtrails in the morning,
Bullhorns at dawn to give us "sheep" a warning.
Yeah ... we're nothing but sheep ... and so is he,

We just got different shepherds,
We use reason to reign ourselves in,
He's a little more "unfettered".

Anyways ... I'm getting side-tracked here,
Could be the situation ... more like the rum or the beer,
But let's be clear ... I saw the offending weapon,
The instigator of the mayhem ...
A five quid kitchen knife they must have got from B&M.
What's that? How do I know? ... well ... I got me one of them.
Bargain, if I say so myself,
Though I've never understood how
You can buy those things straight off the shelf.
Well ... better than guns like they sell in the states,
Lose your shit for a minute and shoot up all your mates!
Imagine that ... a drunken argument and you're shagged,
At least, over here ... you only get stabbed.

Shit! There I go again ... wildly off topic!
But I saw it all with my own two eyes ... they're fucking telescopic!
I got an eye for detail, like I mentioned with the knife,
I suppose you want a description
Of the assailant who took this person's life?
Well ... I'm assuming the victim's dead?
I saw the vicar saying three "Hail Mary's"
And signing crosses over their head.
She's a lovely vicar ... really cares about the community,
She understands this place isn't really
A hot bed of opportunity, she strives for unity,
In a village that's riddled with division,
But she's made it her mission to fill in the cracks
You can her heart break a little each time
The village succumbs to these criminal acts.

Bollocks. I've gone off on one again ...
I must be a right pain, eh officer!?
One of those annoying men that won't cut to the chase?

What's that? Could I do a photo fit of the murderer's face?
So they are dead then?
What a shit state of affairs,
A school night bit of argy-bargy
And now we've got the stuff of nightmares.
No one fucking cares about these working class thoroughfares,
These streets with no shame, just mountains to climb
As The Beacon Hill looks down on us,
Like the privileged do all the time.

What's that? Do I have any useful information?
You would like me to accompany you down to the station?
Good idea boss, gimme coffee and let's speed up my sobriety,
Then I'll tell you everything I saw,
And how the murderer
Is society.

Dying for a Dump in the Car Back From Cheltenham

As I set out from Cheltenham, upon the road for Brum,
I began a conversation with that bit of me called 'my bum'.
For we had journeyed not a mile
And my arse began to scowl,
I knew I should have taken time to empty out my bowel.

My arse began by saying,
"Spoz, you've been a little rash,
You should have stayed a minute more
And let me make a splash"
"Shut up!" I cried as I began to whiff a nasty stench,
"It's a long way back," replied my arse,
"So don't forget to clench".

Well ... the M5 beckoned,
"It's not that far" I reckoned
And suddenly, I didn't feel so concerned,
For the services close to the M50 junction,
Would relieve me of the dump for which I yearned.
As I approached the service station,
My defecating urge had subsided ...
So I drove past ... that's when my arse screamed,
Just about the same time as I did.

"What!" I yelled out,
"You fool!" cried my arse,
"I was saving myself for the services,
Now I'm going to feel like that elephant on 'Blue Peter',
...and guess who poor old Peter Purvis is!"

Well...Worcester came and Worcester went,
The sweat dripped from my brow,

I managed to stop myself 'logging out',
But to this day ... I'm not sure how.
As I flew past the town of Droitwich,
I sensed my marmite motorway's wrath,
Fifteen minutes longer
And I'd be touching cloth.
As my exit – junction 4, rapidly approached,
I felt the outer sanctum of my sphincter being broached,
The turtle's head was peeping out,
There was no going back,
Pretty soon his ample girth,
Would be crawling from my crack.

I pulled up on my drive at last,
Though my efforts were all in vain.
The turtle crept around my pants,
As I was doubled up in pain.
I slumped down onto the toilet ... but it wasn't over yet,
As I laid down another big jobby ...
About the size of a healthy courgette!

So...don't get caught out in your car,
Here's one moral that can be agreed on ...
Don't be a fool with an imminent stool
And have a good shit when you need one.

ACKNOWLEDGEMENTS

This is a list of people who have inspired me, influenced me or helped me in anyway (whether they know it or not). So allow me to say "thank you".

Mama e Papa e la famiglia Esposito
Lola and Poppy (you keep me going!)
Zack, Sabrina, Fran, Tom and Claude xxxxx
Uncle Derek in Zakinthos (yes, comrade!)
Dreadlockalien, Elvis McGonagall, AF Harrold, John Hegley, Ben Folds, Rush, John Cooper Clarke, Attila the Stockbroker, Hollie McNish, Kae Tempest, Polar Bear, Rob Gee, Berko, Andy Craven Griffiths, Longfella, Jimmy Davis, Johnny Fluffypunk, The Antipoet, Pete the Temp, Jodi Anne Bickley, Hannah Teasdale, Bohdan Piasecki, Matt Windle, Holly Winter Hughes, Katherine Priddy (it's been ace to watch you grow!) Jemima Hughes, Helen Gregory, Charley Barnes, Ash Dickinson, Fergus McGonigall, Jamie Thrasivoulou, Jasmine Gardosi, Ayan Aden, Hazel Sealeaf, Lorna Rose, Casey Bailey, Evrah Rose, Joe Cook, Amerah Saleh, Kamil Mahmood, Nafeesa Hamid, Willis the Poet, Hayley Frances, William Gallagher, Steve Pottinger, Dave Pitt and Emma Pursehouse.
The brilliant and irreplaceable Benjamin Zephaniah (RIP UTV)
The lovely Leon Priestnall (RIP mate)
The wonderful Big Bren (RIP mate)
The legend that is David Bowie (RIP)

Stuart Bartholomew and The Verve crew for giving a voice to Brum!
Birmingham, Worcestershire, Shropshire and Staffordshire Libraries,
Scott Tyrell for his ace artwork ... and being a darned good poet too!
My lads in 'Vaseline'.
Jonathan and Writing West Midlands,
Arts Council England (cheers Pete!)
The Word Association CIC.
My lovely 'Bards of Brum' and gang at The Commonwealth Games.

Apples and Snakes especially Jacob and Lisa (and the rest of you obviously!),
The Palace Theatre, Redditch,
The Playhouse Theatre, Cheltenham
Artrix Theatre, Bromsgrove,
MAC Birmingham,
Alice Chambers and everyone at The Rep Birmingham that helped 'Canalligator' come to life.
Authors Abroad (you rock!)
Paul Stringer for his bostin filming and photography.
All the schools I've visited and yet to visit, especially the teachers who have been brilliantly supportive under stress and all the kids who have been ace, even though they thought (and probably still think) "poetry's boring".

...and anyone else who knows me.

ABOUT VERVE POETRY PRESS

Verve Poetry Press is a prize-winning press that focused initially on meeting a local need in Birmingham - a need for the vibrant poetry scene here in Brum to find a way to present itself to the poetry world via publication. Co-founded by Stuart Bartholomew and Amerah Saleh, it now publishes poets from all corners of the UK - poets that speak to the city's varied and energetic qualities and will contribute to its many poetic stories.

Added to this is a colourful pamphlet series, many featuring poets who have performed at our sister festival - and a poetry show series which captures the magic of longer poetry performance pieces by festival alumni such as Polarbear, Suhaiymah Manzoor-Khan and Imogen Stirling.

The press has been voted Most Innovative Publisher at the Saboteur Awards, and has won the Publisher's Award for Poetry Pamphlets at the Michael Marks Awards.

Like the festival, we strive to think about poetry in inclusive ways and embrace the multiplicity of approaches towards this glorious art.

www.vervepoetrypress.com
@VervePoetryPres
mail@vervepoetrypress.com